CURRICULUM AND EVALUATION

S T A N D A R D S

FOR SCHOOL MATHEMATICS
ADDENDA SERIES, GRADES K–6

THIRD-GRADE BOOK

Grace Burton

Douglas Clements

Terrence Coburn

John Del Grande

John Firkins

Jeane Joyner

Miriam A. Leiva

Mary M. Lindquist

Lorna Morrow

Miriam A. Leiva, Series Editor

NATIONAL COUNCIL OF
TEACHERS OF MATHEMATICS

Copyright © 1992 by
THE NATIONAL COUNCIL OF TEACHERS OF MATHEMATICS, INC.
1906 Association Drive, Reston, Virginia 22091-1593
All rights reserved

Third printing 1992

Library of Congress Cataloging-in-Publication Data:

Third-grade book / Grace Burton ... [et al.].
    p.   cm. — (Curriculum and evaluation standards for school
mathematics addenda series. Grades K–6)
    Includes bibliographical references.
    ISBN 0-87353-313-5 (vol.). — ISBN 0-87353-309-7 (set)
    1. Mathematics—Study and teaching (Elementary)   2. Curriculum
evaluation.   I. Burton, Grace M.   II. National Council of Teachers
of Mathematics.   III. Series.
QA135.5.T485 1992
372.7—dc20   91-34131
                                    QA   CIP
                                    135.5
                                    .T485
                                    1992

Photographs are by Patricia Fisher; artwork is by Lynn Gohman and Don Christian.

The publications of the National Council of Teachers of Mathematics present a variety of viewpoints. The views expressed or implied in this publication, unless otherwise noted, should not be interpreted as official positions of the Council.

Printed in the United States of America

FOREWORD

The *Curriculum and Evaluation Standards for School Mathematics* (NCTM 1989a) describes a framework for revising and strengthening school mathematics. This visionary document provides a set of guidelines for K–12 mathematics curricula and for evaluating both the mathematics curriculum and students' progress. It not only addresses what mathematics students should learn but also how they should learn it.

As the document was being developed, it became apparent that supporting publications would be needed to interpret and illustrate how the vision could be translated realistically into classroom practices. A Task Force on the Addenda to the Curriculum and Evaluation Standards for School Mathematics, chaired by Thomas Rowan and composed of Joan Duea, Christian Hirsch, Marie Jernigan, and Richard Lodholz, was appointed by Shirley Frye, then NCTM president. The Task Force's recommendations on the scope and nature of the supporting publications were submitted to the Educational Materials Committee, which subsequently framed the Addenda Project.

Central to the Addenda Project was the formation of three writing teams—consisting of classroom teachers, mathematics supervisors, and university mathematics educators—to prepare a series of publications, the Addenda Series, targeted at mathematics instruction in grades K–6, 5–8, and 9–12. The purpose of the series is to clarify and illustrate the message of the *Curriculum and Evaluation Standards*. The underlying themes of problem solving, reasoning, communication, and connections are woven throughout the materials, as is the view of assessment as a means of guiding instruction. Activities have been field tested by teachers to ensure that they reflect the realities of today's classrooms.

It is envisioned that the Addenda Series will be a source of ideas by teachers as they begin to implement the recommendations in the NCTM *Curriculum and Evaluation Standards*. Individual volumes in the series are appropriate for in-service programs and for preservice courses in teacher education programs.

A project of this magnitude required the efforts and talents of many people over an extended time. Sincerest appreciation is extended to the authors and the editor and to the following teachers who played key roles in developing, revising, and trying out the materials for the *Third-Grade Book*: Angela C. Gardner, Carolyn Lennon, and Debbie Mortimer. Finally, this project would not have materialized without the outstanding technical support supplied by Cynthia Rosso and the NCTM publications staff.

Bonnie H. Litwiller
Addenda Project Coordinator

PREFACE

Something exciting is happening in many elementary school classrooms! A vision of an innovative mathematics program is coming alive. There *is* a shift in emphasis in the teaching and learning of mathematics. Teachers are encouraging children to investigate, discuss, question, and verify. They are focusing on explorations and dialogues. They are using various strategies to assess students' progress. They are making mathematics accessible to all children while exposing them to the value and the beauty of mathematics. Teachers and students are excited, and their enthusiasm is contagious. You can *catch it* when you hear children confidently explaining their solutions to the class, when you see them modeling problems with manipulatives, and when you observe them using a variety of methods and materials to arrive at answers. Some children are working with paper and pencil or with calculators; others are sharpening their estimation and mental math skills. There is noise in these classrooms—the sounds of students actively participating in the class and constructing their own knowledge through experiences that will give them confidence in their own abilities and make them mathematically powerful.

> I remember my own experiences in mathematics in elementary school. The classroom was quiet; all you could hear was the movement of pencils across sheets of paper and an occasional comment from the teacher. I was often bored; work was done in silent isolation, rules were memorized, and many routine problems were worked using rules few of us understood. Mathematics didn't always make sense. It was something that you did in school, mostly with numbers, and that you didn't need outside the classroom.
>
> "Why are we doing this?" my friend whispered.
>
> "Because it's in the book," I replied.
>
> "Do it this way," the teacher would explain while writing another problem on the chalkboard. "When you finish, work the next ten problems in the book."

We must go beyond how we were taught and teach how we wish we had been taught. We must bring to life a vision of what a mathematics classroom should be.

Rationale for Change

These are challenging times for you, the teachers of elementary school mathematics, and for your students. Major reforms in school mathematics are advocated in reports that call for changes in the curriculum, in student and program evaluations, in instruction, and in the classroom environment. These reforms are prompted by the changing needs of our society, which demand that all students become mathematically literate to function effectively in a technological world. A richer mathematics program is also supported by an explosion of new mathematical knowledge—more mathematics has been created in this century than in all our previous history. Research studies on teaching and learning, with emphasis on *how children learn mathematics,* have had a significant impact on current practices and strengthen the case for reform. Advances in technology also dictate changes in content and teaching.

Our students, the citizens of tomorrow, need to learn not only *more* mathematics but also mathematics that is broader in scope. They must have a strong academic foundation to enable them to expand their knowledge, to interpret information, to make reasonable decisions, and to solve increasingly complex problems using various approaches and tools, including calculators and computers. Mathematics instruction must reflect and implement these revised educational goals and increased expectations.

The blueprint for reform is the *Curriculum and Evaluation Standards for School Mathematics* (NCTM 1989a), which identifies a set of standards for the mathematics curriculum in grades K–12 as well as standards for evaluating the quality of programs and students' performance. The *Curriculum and Evaluation Standards* sets forth a bold vision of what mathematics education in grades K–12 should be and describes how mathematics classrooms can fit the vision.

Mathematics as Sense Making

In the past, mathematics classrooms were dominated by instruction and performance of rote procedures "to get the right answer." The *Curriculum and Evaluation Standards* supports the view of school mathematics as a sense-making experience encompassing a wide range of content, instructional approaches, and evaluation techniques.

Four standards are closely woven into content and instruction: mathematics as problem solving, mathematics as communication, mathematics as reasoning, and mathematical connections. These strands are common themes that support all other standards throughout all grade levels.

A primary goal for the study of mathematics is to give children experiences that promote the ability *to solve problems* and that build mathematics from situations generated within the context of everyday experiences. Students are also expected *to make conjectures and conclusions* and *to discuss their reasoning* in words, both written and spoken; with pictures, graphs, and charts; and with manipulatives. Moreover, students learn *to value mathematics* when they *make connections* between topics in mathematics, between the concrete and the abstract, between concepts and skills, and between mathematics and other areas in the curriculum.

The Changing Roles of Students

Previous efforts to reform school mathematics focused primarily on the curriculum; the *Curriculum and Evaluation Standards* also deals with other factors—in particular, students—that affect and are affected by reforms. The role of students is redirected from passive recipients to active participants, from isolated workers to team members, from listeners to investigators and reporters, and from timid followers to intrepid explorers and risk takers. They are asked to develop, discuss, create, model, validate, and investigate to learn mathematics.

Many people, including students, believe that mathematics is for the privileged few. It is time to dispel that myth. All children, regardless of sex, socioeconomic background, language, race, or ethnic origin, can and must succeed in school mathematics. With proper instruction, encouragement, and high expectations, *all* students can do mathematics.

Your Role in Implementing the Standards

All elementary school teachers are teachers of mathematics. Thus, your role is to build your students' self-confidence and nurture their natural curiosity; to challenge them with rich problems through which they will learn to value mathematics and appreciate the order and beauty of mathematics; to provide them with a strong foundation for further study; and to encourage their mathematical ability and power.

The elementary school years are crucial in a child's cognitive and affective development, and you are the central figure. You structure classroom experiences to implement the curriculum and create a supportive

My mom thought that we popped corn just for fun, until I showed her the story I wrote about how we guessed and measured in math class.

When the class drew and classified flags of the world, Antonio noticed that the flags of Cuba and Puerto Rico were identical in design but with colors reversed.

If I had 12 blocks, I could make a set of 4 stairs with 2 blocks left over.

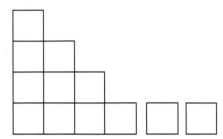

My box has two square faces. The other four faces are rectangles.

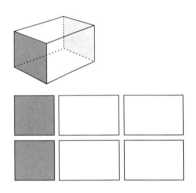

Box faces

Since the total number of circles in the third term is 3 x 3, or 9, then I know that there are 10 x 10, or 100, circles in the tenth term.

environment for learning to take place. In most activities you are the guide, the coach, the facilitator, and the instigator of mathematical explorations.

♦ You give children the gift of self-confidence. Through your careful grouping, astute questions, appropriate tasks, and realistic expectations, each student can experience success.

♦ Long after they forget childhood events, your students will remember you. Your excitement and interest permeate the room and stimulate their appreciation for mathematics.

♦ Through your classroom practices, you promote mathematical thinking, reasoning, and understanding.

♦ You lay the foundation on which further study will take place. You give students multiple strategies and tools to solve problems. The questions you ask and the problems you pose can capture your students' imagination, arouse their curiosity, and encourage their creativity.

♦ You facilitate the building of their knowledge by giving them interesting problems to solve, which leads to the development of concepts and important mathematical ideas.

♦ Rules, algorithms, and formulas emerge from student explorations guided by you, the teacher of mathematics.

Instructional Tools and the Standards

In order to implement the curriculum envisioned in the *Curriculum and Evaluation Standards,* we must carefully select and creatively use instructional tools. The textbook is only one of many important teaching resources. Children's development of concepts is fostered by their extensive use of physical materials to represent and describe mathematical ideas.

Calculators and computers are essential instructional tools at all levels. Through the appropriate use of these tools, students are able to solve realistic problems, investigate patterns, explore procedures, and focus on the steps to solve problems instead of on tedious computations.

Implementing the Evaluation Standards

Evaluation must be an integral part of teaching. A primary component of instruction is an ongoing assessment of what goes on in our classrooms. This information helps us make decisions about what we teach and how we teach it, about students' progress and feelings, and about our mathematics program.

The *Curriculum and Evaluation Standards* advocates many changes in curriculum, in instruction, and in the roles of students and teachers. None of these changes are more important than those related to evaluation. We must learn to use a variety of assessment instruments and not depend on pencil-and-paper tests alone. Tools such as observations, interviews, projects, reports, portfolios, diaries, and tests provide a more complete picture of what children understand and are able to use. Knowing what questions to ask is a skill we must develop.

When we test, we send a message about what we think is important. Because we encourage reasoning and communicating mathematically, we practice these skills. Because manipulatives and calculators are valuable tools for learning, we promote their use in the classroom. Because we want children to experience cooperative problem solving, we provide opportunities for group activities. *Not only must we evaluate what we want children to learn, but also how we want them to learn it.*

You and This Book

This booklet is part of the Curriculum and Evaluation for School Mathematics Addenda Series, Grades K–6. This series was designed to illustrate the standards and to help you translate them into classroom practice through—

♦ sample lessons and discussions that focus on the development of concepts;

♦ activities that connect models and manipulatives with concepts and with mathematical representations;

♦ problems that exemplify the use and integration of technology;

♦ teaching strategies that promote students' reasoning;

♦ approaches to evaluate students' progress;

♦ techniques to improve instruction.

In this booklet, both traditional and new topics are explored in four areas: Patterns, Number Sense and Operations, Making Sense of Data, and Geometry and Spatial Sense.

You will find classic third-grade activities that have been infused with an investigative flavor. These experiences include drawing geometric figures by using Logo; exploring properties of solids by looking at their nets, faces, and vertices; collecting, organizing, and interpreting data; developing estimation strategies; finding patterns and describing them numerically and geometrically; and using calculators to explore number sequences. You will also encounter a variety of problems and questions to explore with your third graders. Margin notes give you additional information on the activities and on such topics as student self-confidence, evaluation, and grouping. Connections to science, language arts, social studies, and other areas in the curriculum are made throughout. Supporting statements from the *Curriculum and Evaluation Standards* appear as margin notes.

Change is an ongoing process that takes time and courage. It is not easy to go beyond comfort and security to try new things. As you use this book, pick and choose at will, and sample alternative approaches and ideas for instruction and assessment. Savor the freedom of change. All the documents in the world will not effect change in the classrooms; *only you can.*

The Challenge and the Vision

"I wonder why...?"

"What would happen if...?"   "Tell me about your pattern."

"Can you do it another way?"   "Our group has a different solution."

These inviting words give students the freedom to be creative, the confidence to solve problems, and the power to do mathematics. When you give your students the opportunity to construct their own knowledge, you are opening the doors of mathematics to *all* young learners.

This is the challenge. This is the vision.

Miriam A. Leiva, Editor
K–6 Addenda Series

I think that there are about 400 beans in the jar because there are about 20 beans on the bottom layer and about 20 layers of beans.

$$\begin{array}{r} 20 \\ \times\ 20 \\ \hline 400 \end{array}$$

We asked all third-grade students and found out that more of them liked french fries better than mashed potatoes.

French fries	85
Mashed potatoes	28

BIBLIOGRAPHY

National Council of Teachers of Mathematics. *Curriculum and Evaluation Standards for School Mathematics Addenda Series, Grades K–6*, edited by Miriam A. Leiva. Reston, Va.: The Council, 1991.

———. *Curriculum and Evaluation Standards for School Mathematics Addenda Series, Grades 5–8*, edited by Frances R. Curcio. Reston, Va.: The Council, 1991.

———. *Curriculum and Evaluation Standards for School Mathematics Addenda Series, Grades 9–12*, edited by Christian R. Hirsch. Reston, Va.: The Council, 1991.

———. *Curriculum and Evaluation Standards for School Mathematics.* Reston, Va.: The Council, 1989a.

———. *New Directions for Elementary School Mathematics.* 1989 Yearbook, edited by Paul Trafton. Reston, Va.: The Council, 1989b.

———. *Professional Standards for Teaching Mathematics.* Reston, Va.: The Council, 1991.

National Research Council. *Everybody Counts: A Report to the Nation on the Future of Mathematics Education.* Washington, D.C.: National Academy Press, 1989.

ACKNOWLEDGMENTS

At a time when the mathematics community was looking for directions on implementing the *Curriculum and Evaluation Standards for School Mathematics,* a group of dedicated professionals agreed to serve on the NCTM Elementary Addenda Project.

The task of editing and writing for this series has been challenging and rewarding. Selecting, testing, writing, and editing, as we attempted to translate the message of the *Standards* into classroom practices, proved to be a monumental and ambitious task. It could not have been done without the dedication and hard work of the authors, the teachers who reviewed and field tested the activities, and the editorial team.

My appreciation is extended to the main authors for each topic:

Grace Burton	Number Sense and Operations
Terrence Coburn	Patterns
John Del Grande and Lorna Morrow	Geometry and Spatial Sense
Mary M. Lindquist	Making Sense of Data

Our colleagues in the classrooms, Angela Gardner, Carolyn Lennon, and Debbie Mortimer, are thanked for giving us the unique perspective of teachers and children.

A special note of gratitude is owed to the individuals who served both as writers and as the editorial panel: Douglas Clements, John Firkins, and Jeane Joyner.

The editor also gratefully acknowledges the strong support of Bonnie Litwiller, Coordinator of the Addenda Project, and the assistance of Cynthia Rosso and the NCTM production staff for their guidance and help through the process of planning and producing this series of books.

The greatest reward for all who have contributed to this effort will be the knowledge that the ideas presented here have been implemented in elementary school classrooms, that these ideas have made realities out of visions, and that they have fostered improved mathematics programs for all children.

Miriam A. Leiva

PATTERNS

Working with patterns is an exciting and motivating experience for children and a significant form of problem solving. Understanding and using patterns and relationships lead students toward algebraic thinking. Recording and analyzing data to discover patterns build students' confidence in their ability to do mathematics independently, without the need for constant confirmation from the teacher. At each repetition of a simple pattern, children are validating, for themselves, the pattern that they have discovered.

Organizing data in a table is an essential mathematical skill. It helps children to see relationships within patterns and eventually to generalize these relationships to form a rule.

In previous grades, children became familiar with both repeating patterns and growing patterns. They began to associate and record numbers on pictures of patterns as a way to record and report their observations. The following third-grade activities focus on creating and using tables as a technique for analyzing and reporting patterns. Numbers are used to identify order in a sequence of data. To help students see the relationship between the terms of the sequence and the pattern, ask them questions such as these:

Can you tell me how we got the number for the third term? What is the fourth term? What do you do to get the fifth term?

In which term did you discover a pattern? What is the tenth term?

Children need many experiences with patterns; these activities are but a sample. If children develop the habit of finding, inventing, and using patterns to solve problems, they will have taken a significant step toward developing mathematical power.

Children might make many different observations when looking at this marble pattern: "Each term has one more row of marbles." "Each new row of marbles is at the bottom of the pile. It has one more marble than the previous bottom row." "Each pile is a triangle. There are as many rows of marbles in the triangle as there are marbles in the bottom row."

PATTERNS ON THE HUNDREDS CHART

Get ready. The purpose of this activity is to have children recognize and describe patterns on a hundreds chart.

You will need an overhead transparency of a hundreds chart or a large hundreds chart for display. Each child will need at least two copies of the chart, crayons, and markers or counters in at least two colors. You may wish to incorporate calculators into this activity.

Get going. Give each child a copy of the chart and a supply of counters. Make the patterns on the overhead transparency or the display chart as the children work at their desks. Explore the chart with the class and ask them what patterns they see. For example, a child might say, "I see a pattern in the third row: 31, 32, 33,..., 40. The ones digit goes up by 1 and the tens digit stays the same until you get to 40."

Introduce other patterns. For example, have everyone place counters on the multiples of 3: 3, 6, 9,.... Ask the children to describe the pattern. Ask them to close their eyes while you move one or more counters on the display chart.

Open your eyes and tell me which counters I moved. How do you know?

1	2	3	4	5	6	7	8	9	10
11	12	13	14	15	16	17	18	19	20
21	22	23	24	25	26	27	28	29	30
31	32	33	34	35	36	37	38	39	40
41	42	43	44	45	46	47	48	49	50
51	52	53	54	55	56	57	58	59	60
61	62	63	64	65	66	67	68	69	70
71	72	73	74	75	76	77	78	79	80
81	82	83	84	85	86	87	88	89	90
91	92	93	94	95	96	97	98	99	100

Hundreds charts afford you a quick way to assess a child's knowledge of a variety of factual information. Review place value, number facts, and mental computation. Because you can see many students' responses at once, you will be able to note those children who place markers with confidence and those who hesitate.

Explore with the class the patterns made with other numbers and their multiples, using the chart. Then pair or group the students and assign each group a number. Have them cover the assigned number and its multiples with counters on the chart. Repeat the group activity with other numbers. Ask the students to discuss the patterns they find. At the end of the lesson, have the children choose their favorite pattern and color it on their hundreds charts.

Keep going. Explore patterns with the children in different ways.

Ask the students to describe the spatial pattern that results when they place counters on 11 and the multiples of 11. [An oblique or diagonal line of nine counters from 11 to 99]

If you place a counter on all the squares where the digit 5 occurs, how many of the 100 squares will have counters on them? [19] *What does the pattern look like? Repeat with other digits.*

Do you always get the same result? Why or why not? Can you predict what the pattern will look like if you cover all the 8s?

Have the children skip count by 2s and then by 3s, marking the multiples of 2 with one color counter and the multiples of 3 with a different color counter.

Which numbers have two colors on them? [6, 12, 18, 25,..., 96] *Why?* [They are multiples of both 2 and 3; that is, they are multiples of 6.]

Have the students start with 3 and count on by 5s (3, 8, 13, 18,...).

What is the pattern in the units digit? Can you use a table or an organized list to help you find out? Why does this pattern occur?

Eighty-three is a number in this sequence. What number comes before 83 in the sequence? How do you know?

For each of the following patterns, have the students tell by which number you are counting:

8, 14, 20, 26, 32, 44, 50,...
9, 13, 17, 21, 25, 29, 33,...
27, 41, 55, 69, 83,...

Activities in which students cover the multiples of two or more numbers on one chart are readiness experiences for work with common multiples.

Have the students find the following numbers in the chart: 7, 16, 25, 34, 43, 52, 61.

Ask them to describe the visual pattern. ["Each number is one square down, one square to the left."] Discuss the numerical pattern. ["Nine more, or counting on by 9s." "Nine more is 10 more minus 1."] Have them add the digits and discuss their observations. ["The sum is always 7."] Ask them to explain why this would be true and to find other similar sequences.

Assess children's understanding by asking, If I cover a number by moving my counter 1 to the right (1 left, 1 up, 1 down, 1 up and to the left, and so on), what is its relationship to the previous number?

Have the students cover the following numbers on the chart: 2, 13, 24, 35, 46, 57, 68, 79.

Ask them to describe the pattern spatially and numerically. ["Each number is one square down, one square to the right."] ["Eleven more"] Is there a pattern in the sum or the difference of the digits? Have them describe and explain their discoveries.

Have the students add the digits of consecutive numbers, for example, 20, 21, 22, 23,..., 29: 2 + 0 = 2, 2 + 1 = 3, 2 + 2 = 4,....

What pattern do you see? Does it hold in every row of the chart?

Ask the children to choose numbers from each row along a diagonal, for example, 4, 15, 26, 37, 48, 59,.... Have them add their digits: 4, 1 + 5 = 6, 2 + 6 = 8, 3 + 7 = 10,....

Is there a pattern? Describe it.

As a variation, use charts that are organized differently, such as the ones shown at the right. Ask the children to investigate these charts and to describe the patterns they see. Have the students create problems for their classmates to solve using these charts. Problem posing is just as important as problem solving.

DESCRIBING PATTERNS NUMERICALLY

Get ready. The purposes of this activity are to analyze, extend, and describe patterns numerically.

Students will need a copy of the Growing Patterns worksheet (p. 8) and manipulatives such as pattern blocks, circular counters, or paper cut-outs.

Get going. Show this pattern using concrete objects and encourage your students to describe it.

What changes as we go from one term to the next? What stays the same?

Ask a student to place additional figures to extend the pattern. Ask the children to describe the pattern and tell what would come next.

Have the students work in groups of two or three to extend a pattern that you provide (give them three terms). Ideas for patterns are given on the Growing Patterns worksheet and at the right. Encourage the children to use manipulatives to copy and extend the patterns for three or four more terms. Have them record the number of objects in each term.

Have each group present one pattern to the class. Ask them to describe everything they see in their patterns (students may use numerical, spatial, and their own language). Invite the class to contribute their ideas.

Keep going. To encourage communication, have the children share patterns with a partner. Each partner makes a pattern with manipulatives, records the pattern in symbols on paper, and then removes the manipulatives. The partners switch papers and try to create a manipulative pattern that embodies the symbols their partner recorded.

Different patterns will emerge for some of the activities if different charts are used.

0	1	2	3	4	5	6	7	8	9
10	11	12	13	14	15	16	17	18	19
20	21	22	23	24	25	26	27	28	29
30	31	32	33	34	35	36	37	38	39
40	41	42	43	44	45	46	47	48	49
50	51	52	53	54	55	56	57	58	59
60	61	62	63	64	65	66	67	68	69
70	71	72	73	74	75	76	77	78	79
80	81	82	83	84	85	86	87	88	89
90	91	92	93	94	95	96	97	98	99

1	2	3	4	5	6
7	8	9	10	11	12
13	14	15	16	17	18
19	20	21	22	23	24
31	32	33	34	35	36
37	38	39	40	41	42
43	44	45	46	47	48
49	50	51	52	53	54
55	56	57	58	59	60
61	62	63	64	65	66
67	68	69	70	71	72
73	74	75	76	77	78
79	80	81	82	83	84
85	86	87	88	89	90
91	92	93	94	95	96

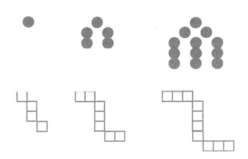

Use concrete materials whenever possible. Inexpensive and accessible manipulatives such as beans, shells, blocks, chips, and geometric shapes are appropriate materials for modeling mathematical concepts.

One partner makes a pattern and records the pattern by writing the number of objects in the pattern:

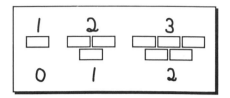

Then he or she removes the manipulatives, leaving only the written numerals:

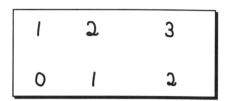

A pattern can be described with numbers in several ways. The labels in this example are one of the many possible numerical descriptions of the pattern.

The other partner then creates with different manipulatives a pattern that follows the same numerical pattern:

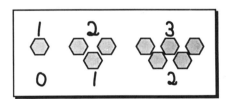

Ask the students to count and record the total number of objects in each of the pattern's terms. Save the patterns and the data for other activities.

Have the students describe and record numerically the patterns on the Growing Patterns worksheet. By doing this activity, students bridge from the pictorial to the symbolic level.

MAKING TABLES

Get ready. The purposes of this activity are to help students record number patterns in tables and use these tables to explore the patterns further. The activities focus on the term and on the total number of objects.

You will need pencils, strips of graph paper, and manipulatives or drawing paper. Use the patterns created in previous activities.

Get going. Start with a simple pictorial pattern on the chalkboard. Draw four or five terms of the pattern and have the class observe and discuss

◆　　　◆　　　◆　　　◆　　　◆　　　◆　　　◆　　　◆

it as described in the previous activity. Ask the students how they would keep track of these patterns. Suggest numbering each term in the pattern. Do they see how the numbers could help them? Use the students' language as much as possible. Discuss the idea that numbering helps us keep track of the pattern.

Have the students explore and describe the square numbers pattern:

Square numbers	o	o o o o	o o o o o o o o o	o o o o o o o o o o o o o o o o
Term	1	2	3	4
Total number of circles	1	4	9	16

Encourage the students to use the numerical information in the table to extend their knowledge of the pattern.

Can you tell how many circles would be needed in term 7? How do you know? How many circles would be needed in term 20?

Could one of the terms have a total of 50 circles? Explain.

Explore another pattern with the class:

	o	o o o	o o o o o	o o o o o o o
Term	1	2	3	4
Total number of circles	1	3	5	?

How many circles are in term 4? [Some students may describe term 4 as having two or more than the previous term; others may say that there are 4 + 3 circles.]

How many circles are in term 6? Explain.

How does the term number help you determine the answer?

What is the difference between the total number of circles in the first and second terms? The second and third? Is there a pattern in these differences?

Lead the class in investigating the patterns in the quadrinumbers and recording the information on a table.

Quadrinumbers

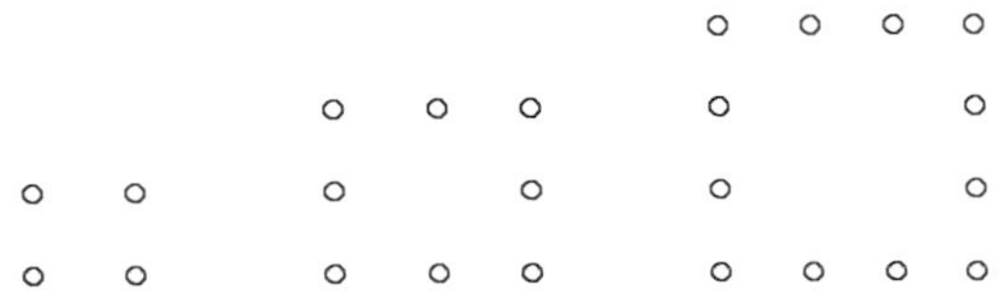

How many circles are in the tenth term? Which term has 36 circles?

Encourage the students to compare and contrast this pattern with the square numbers.

Keep going. Have the students make tables to describe numerically the patterns they created in the Describing Patterns activity. Pose additional problems for the students to solve by finding patterns and making tables.

Frank is building a set of stairs out of blocks.

How many blocks are needed for 4 stairs? [10]

How many does he need for 12 stairs? [78]

How many stairs can he make if exactly 36 blocks are available?

If you have 50 blocks, how many different sets of stairs can you make?
[There are many answers, e.g., 9 stairs with 5 blocks left over, 2 stairs
with 47 blocks left over.]

CALCULATOR SEQUENCE

Get ready. The purpose of this activity is to have students reproduce and
analyze arithmetic sequences by using a calculator.

You will need paper, pencils, and at least one calculator for each group
of two to three students. Children will be repeatedly adding numbers.
They can simply add the same number (e.g., 2 [+] 2 [=] 4 [+] 2 [=] 6 [+]
2 [=] 8). You might, however, have them use the arithmetic constant
capability for addition that most calculators have. You can test your
calculator by pressing

$$2 \boxed{+} \boxed{=} \boxed{=} \boxed{=} \boxed{=} \boxed{=} \dots \text{ or}$$

$$0 \boxed{+} 2 \boxed{=} \boxed{=} \boxed{=} \boxed{=} \boxed{=} \dots \text{ or}$$

$$2 \boxed{+} \boxed{+} \boxed{+} \boxed{+} \dots.$$

If one of these produces the desired successive display of 2, 4, 6, 8,
10,..., your calculator has an arithmetic constant.

Get going. Have the students key in any number on their calculators, say
17. Select any one-digit number, say 6, and have them skip count with
their calculators and record the sequence as it appears in the display.
For example, 17 [+] 6 [=] [=] [=] .... Have the students note the digits in
the ones place.

Will 137 be in the sequence? How would you find out?

Such activities lay the foundation for the multiplication and the division algorithms. Practice skip counting by other numbers on the calculator and record the sequence. Have the children record the first five numbers of each sequence on the chalkboard and challenge other students to find the next number of the sequence. Have the students explain how they determined each successive number (e.g., by subtracting to find the constant and then adding this number to the last term).

Write a sequence of five numbers, such as 27, 41, 55, 69, and 83, on the chalkboard.

Did they result from skip counting? How do you know?

Write another number, such as 181, and ask whether or not this number is in the sequence of numbers. Show the students how to reproduce this sequence of numbers on their calculators:

27 $\boxed{+}$ 14 $\boxed{=}$ $\boxed{=}$ $\boxed{=}$ $\boxed{=}$

Repeatedly pressing the $\boxed{=}$ (or $\boxed{+}$) key causes the sequence to appear on the display. Counting the number of times the $\boxed{=}$ key is pressed helps keep track of where in the sequence 181 falls. [181 is the twelfth number in the sequence.] Give further practice in creating a sequence on the calculator; for example, 18 $\boxed{+}$ 5 $\boxed{=}$ $\boxed{=}$ $\boxed{=}$ ... gives this sequence: 18, 23, 28, 33, 38,...

Keep going. The following is a sample of the kinds of problems you might pose:

Is 222 in the sequence 11, 22, 33, 44,...? What is the seventh term? The seventeenth term? How do you know?

Look at this sequence: 51, 61, 71, 81, 91,.... Is 123 one of the numbers in this sequence? 1111? 910? Explain.

Reproduce this sequence on the calculator: 13, 94, 175, 256, 337,.... The number 1552 is in this sequence. What term in the sequence is 1552?

Use the following clues to reproduce the sequence on the calculator: The fourth number in the sequence is 95. Each number in the sequence is 12 more than the previous number. What is the first number? [59] The twentieth? [287] (Repeat this activity with repeated subtraction; that is, reproduce sequences such as 1000, 973, 946, 919,....)

Play the following game in which you share one calculator with your partner. Start at 50. In turn, subtract any one-digit number except 0. The player to reach 0 first wins. Can you find a strategy to win? Does it matter who goes first? Suppose the person who first reaches 0 loses; how might this change your strategy?

Repeat the activity but start with different numbers. Discuss the winning strategies.

A major goal of mathematics instruction is to help children develop the belief that they have the power to do mathematics and that they have control over their own success or failure. (NCTM 1989a, p. 29)

Students might also use a Logo program to print the term number and the number of elements. The real benefit of such a program is the ease with which students can explore "What if...?" questions by changing the starting number and the amount of change.

```
TO PATTERN
MAKE "TERM 1
MAKE "N 27
MAKE "CHANGE 14
REPEAT 20 [PATTERN2]
END
TO PATTERN2
PR SE :TERM :N
MAKE "TERM :TERM + 1
MAKE "N :N + :CHANGE
END
```

In this program, the first term is 27 and each term increases by 14. There are twenty terms generated.

GROWING PATTERNS

Extend the patterns two more terms. Record.

1.

2.

3.

4.

5.

6.

NUMBER SENSE AND OPERATIONS

When children have number sense, they understand not only the relationships between numbers but also the effects of arithmetical operations on numbers. They exhibit confidence in their answers and willingness to investigate new situations.

Number sense develops over many years, and there may be a wide disparity between the concepts and skills of your third-grade students. The understanding they possess will be fostered if they model numbers in many ways and use numbers to describe real-world situations.

Research over the past few decades has demonstrated that children learn best when they are actively investigating, discussing, and reporting questions of interest. Activities in this section encourage active learning and focus on estimation and multiplication.

STREETS AND AVENUES

Get ready. The purpose of this activity is to have children explore multiplication as an array model. Each group of students needs toothpicks, glue, and paper and a pencil for recording.

Get going. Have the children use toothpicks and glue to build maps showing the streets and the avenues of a small town (where streets intersect avenues at right angles) and use a marker to indicate where stoplights are needed.

How many crossing points for stoplights can you make with two (three, four, five,...) *toothpicks?* Have the students use toothpicks to make maps to show the possible arrangements.

Giving students opportunities to explore interesting problems, applications, and situations does not guarantee that they will make appropriate connections; it is inevitable that some students might lose sight of the important mathematical ideas that underlie any activity. They need to be encouraged and helped to reflect on their explorations and summarize concepts, relationships, processes, and facts that have emerged from their discussions. (NCTM 1989a, p. 103)

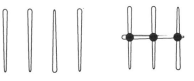

Maps with four toothpicks

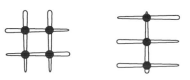

0 stoplights   3 stoplights

4 stoplights   3 stoplights

Operation sense interacts with number sense and enables students to make thoughtful decisions about the reasonableness of results. (NCTM 1989a, p. 41)

Can you arrange four toothpicks so that there would be no stoplights? [Yes] *One stoplight?* [No]

What is the largest number of stoplights you can have? [4]

Help the students organize their findings in a table by recording the number of streets, avenues, and stoplights needed with four toothpicks.

Keep going. This activity provides the students an opportunity to use manipulative materials to investigate products and factors in rectangular arrays. They can also use a pictorial model by drawing line segments and counting points of intersection. Suggest that different groups explore with different numbers of toothpicks. Have them record the maps and organize the data numerically in a table. Relate to multiplication facts.

Number of toothpicks	Number of streets	Number of avenues	Number of stoplights		Multiplication facts
4	4	0	0		$4 \times 0 = 0$
4	3	1	3		$3 \times 1 = 3$
4	2	2	4		$2 \times 2 = 4$
4	1	3	3		$1 \times 3 = 3$
4	0	4	0		$0 \times 4 = 0$

BUNCHES OF BEANS

In this activity, students estimate the number of beans in each jar. The different sizes of beans encourage students to use proportional thinking in estimating the quantity in other jars.

Get ready. The purpose of this activity is to engage students in a series of estimation tasks to develop estimation strategies and a better sense of the reasonableness of results.

Set aside a space in your classroom to display the question of the week and the student responses. In the same area, place a transparent jar filled with dry beans. In subsequent weeks you can vary this activity by using several identical transparent jars or various kinds of dry beans, marbles, or other objects of different sizes.

Estimation interacts with number sense and spatial sense to help children develop insights into concepts and procedures, flexibility in working with numbers and measurements, and an awareness of reasonable results. (NCTM 1989a, p. 36)

Get going. Each Monday, post a question for the week, such as, How many lima beans are in the jar?

Encourage the students to estimate the number and show how they arrived at the estimate. At the end of the week, discuss the set of answers received. Graph them with sticky squares. Ask questions such as the following:

Were some estimates near each other? What was the smallest estimate? The largest?

What number were most estimates near (if any)?

Have the children open the jar and count the beans. Were most of the estimates close to the correct answer?

Discuss the students' strategies for estimation. The students may begin estimating by mentally grouping the objects into tens and hundreds. This should be encouraged, especially since it reinforces place-value concepts.

Keep going. Provide several identical jars, each with beans of a different size. Keep the jars of beans from previous weeks' investigations in the question area along with a file of the corresponding data. These will encourage students to use their earlier estimates and counts as they make their new predictions. Vary the size of the containers and the contents throughout the year. Consider making a small group of students responsible for counting the objects and putting them in the containers. They should record the number, but keep it a secret until everyone has made all the estimates.

POPCORN PREDICTIONS

Get ready. The purpose of this activity is to help students apply their estimation skills and develop a better sense of the relative magnitude of numbers.

Make a transparency of the Popcorn Grids blackline master (p. 16) and cut it in half. Divide the class into groups and give each group a copy of Popcorn Predictions (p. 17), a copy of the 2 x 5 grid from the Popcorn Grids master, and a half cup of popcorn kernels in a paper cup. Have available scales, various containers for the popped corn (jars, paper bags in at least two sizes, and cans), scoops, bowls, a hot-air popper, and cookie sheets or large pieces of clean paper to catch the container overflow. Since they will be eating the popcorn later, make sure that the children wash their hands.

This lesson includes many science concepts. Connections between mathematical topics and language arts are also featured in this activity.

Estimates focus on approximate answers rather than on exact ones. By encouraging students to give responses that include a range, say "between 80 and 90," rather than an exact number, say "87," you will help them to focus on appropriate responses and recognize that estimates do not have to be exact to be useful.

Get going. Give each group of children a set of the materials. Tell them to guess how many kernels there are in their group's container.

Discuss how they might estimate in a systematic way without actually counting the kernels. One way is to count out ten or twenty kernels, and then estimate the number in the cup. Another strategy is to use a grid to help estimate. On the overhead projector, show the transparency picturing popcorn kernels. Then place the 2 x 5 grid on top of it. Ask the students if determining how many kernels are in one rectangle will help them in estimating the total number. Discuss the strategies they invent. Repeat the estimation by placing popcorn kernels randomly on the overhead projector and using the 2 x 5 grid. Discuss whether the strategies are always applicable. What would happen if the popcorn were not evenly spaced?

Have the students use their grid paper to make an estimate of the number of kernels their group has by pouring the kernels onto the grid paper and spreading them out to cover the paper. Students within each group should agree on an estimate. They should record this estimate on their copies of Popcorn Predictions.

Have the groups share their estimates and demonstrate and discuss how they arrived at them.

Have the students make lists of adjectives to describe popped and unpopped corn.

Ask the students if they think that the weight of the kernels before and after popping will be the same. Have them estimate the size of the container needed to hold the popped kernels from one-half cup of popcorn, the time it will take to pop the kernels, and the number of kernels that will not pop. Have them record their estimates on their worksheet. Do the experiment and discuss their findings.

Why does popcorn pop? [Corn seeds contain moisture that turns to steam when heated. The expanding steam cracks the shell.]

Why does the weight change? [The popped corn weighs less because it loses moisture when the steam escapes.]

Keep going. You may wish to extend this activity in several ways:

Have the students compare the popping time and the popping success rate of several brands of popcorn and graph the results.

Do all brands of popcorn pop the same? If you started with one-fourth cup of kernels, how many cups of popcorn would you get for each brand? How many kernels remain unpopped from each batch? How do the results of your experiment compare with the results of the June 1989 Consumer's Report *article on popcorn and popcorn poppers?*

Encourage the students to determine their preferences for corn popped in an oil popper, a microwave oven, or a hot-air popper. They might graph the results of the survey or write a report for the school newspaper or display their findings on the wall outside the classroom.

Challenge the students to find a strategy for determining the weight of a single kernel of corn.

NEWSPAPER SCAVENGER HUNT

Get ready. The purpose of this activity is to have students develop an awareness of the many ways they use numbers in their daily lives.

Materials needed include a newspaper, glue, crayons, and a copy of Newspaper Scavenger Hunt (p.18) for each group of children.

Get going. Give each group a set of materials. Remind them to work together to complete the task. As they find each item, they should cut it out and glue it next to its description on the Newspaper Scavenger Hunt recording sheet.

Keep going. After all the teams have found all the items, you may wish to extend the activity. Some suggestions follow:

Have the students classify the numbers they found into two or more groups by circling the numbers with different colored crayons. When they have done so, ask them to explain the basis of their sorting.

Have the students write a paragraph on how numbers are used in their own lives.

In their mathematics journals, ask students to write about the popcorn lesson, describing the different activities within the lesson. Ask them to reflect on how they might improve their estimation skills.

When mathematical ideas are also connected to everyday experiences, both in and out of school, children become aware of the usefulness of mathematics.
(NCTM 1989a, p. 32)

Building students' ability to think independently helps them sense that they are controlling and creating mathematics.

Have each team develop another scavenger hunt using newspapers, textbooks, or library materials. Students should be instructed not to cut up the books, but to record the book title and the page where the number was found. Have them exchange the new worksheets and repeat the activity with the student-generated "hunts." Students could also develop scavenger hunts for numbers in history, literature, science, and other areas.

USING A DATA BANK

Get ready. The purpose of this activity is to have students generate and solve word problems using realistic data.

Give each group of two students a copy of the Data Bank (p. 19).

Get going. With the whole class, discuss the data base and brainstorm about problems that could be generated from that data base.

Challenge the students to create problems that contain two or more operations. When the children have written the problems, have them trade their sheets with their partners, estimate the answers, and use calculators to solve the problems. You may wish to have the students write and solve their problems on the overhead projector or at the chalkboard. Have the students edit their problems and write them on individual file cards for sharing with other classes or for placing in a mathematics center.

Make connections to science by relating the data bank to the study of energy and calories.

Follow-up discussions are perhaps the most valuable part of this type of activity. They should help students clarify their ideas and write more intelligibly. Ask the students to answer the questions, "What makes a good problem?" and "Why are some problems more interesting than others?" Encourage the children to defend their answers.

Keep going. There are many ways to extend this activity.

Encourage the students to collect similar data from cereal boxes or cookbooks at home and to construct another data bank.

Have them plan a meal and estimate how many calories it contains. How many calories do they need in a day?

Provide restaurant menus and pose problems with several answers, such as "If you receive $2.15 in change, what did you buy and how much money did you give the waiter?" Emphasize students' explanations and reasoning.

TURTLE TRACKS

Get ready. The purpose of this activity is to have children examine and apply the repeated addition model of multiplication. This model also provides readiness experiences for division.

Students should learn to use the computer as a tool for processing information and performing calculations to investigate and solve problems. (NCTM 1989a, p. 8)

You will need at least one computer and Logo software.

Assign the children to groups according to the number of computers available. Choose one child to be the first keyboard leader in each group and establish a schedule that allows every student equal access to the keyboard.

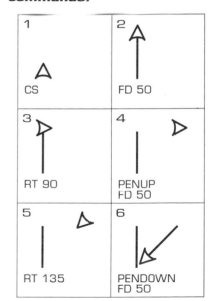

Get going. Have the keyboard leader clear the screen before beginning, then display the following commands:

REPEAT 5 [FD 8]
RT 180

What happened on the screen?

Encourage the children to express the turtle's motion in their own words.

How many steps will the turtle need to get back to the starting place?
[8 + 8 + 8 + 8 + 8 + 8 or 5 × 8 or 8 × 5 or 40]

Discuss with the class Logo commands, such as FD 40, that would return the turtle to its starting point. Have the students check their answers on the computer.

Clear the screen and have the students repeat the activity by using other command sets:

1. REPEAT 6 [FD 8]   2. REPEAT 4 [FD 9]
   RT 180   RT 180

You may wish to reverse the problem by giving the number of turtle steps and having the students give the corresponding multiplication facts or REPEAT commands. Discuss the Logo command FD 32.

Challenge the students to find all the possible REPEAT commands equivalent to FD 32. Have them explain their strategies for finding different solutions and justify each solution.

Possible answers for 32:   Justification:

    REPEAT 1 [FD 32]   1 × 32 = 32
    REPEAT 2 [FD 16]   2 × 16 = 32
    REPEAT 4 [FD 8]   4 × 8 = 32
    REPEAT 8 [FD 4]   8 × 4 = 32
    REPEAT 16 [FD 2]   16 × 2 = 32
    REPEAT 32 [FD 1]   32 × 1 = 32

Keep going. Have the students find other numbers, such as 72, that generate many possible solutions or REPEAT commands (72 is a composite with many factors). Are there some numbers that the turtle can reach in only one way, only two ways, or only three ways? What number less than 100 has the maximum number of solutions? What number has the least? Why?

In Logo, an on-screen "turtle" responds to instructions to draw geometric figures.
FORWARD 50 (FD 50) *instructs the turtle to move forward 50 "turtle steps" in whatever direction it is pointing. Other commands include the following:*
RIGHT 90 (RT 90): *Rotate 90 degrees to the right.*
PENUP (PU): *Put the pen up, so that a path is not drawn.*
PENDOWN (PD): *Put the pen down, so that a path is drawn.*
HT: *Hide the turtle.*
ST: *Show the turtle.*
Commands to clear the screen differ; try CS, DRAW, or CG. *This sequence illustrates some of these commands.*

POPCORN GRIDS

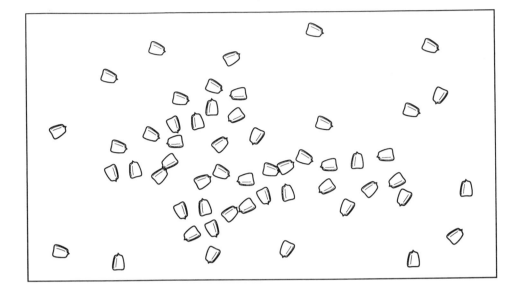

POPCORN PREDICTIONS

I. MEASURE OUT ONE-HALF CUP OF POPCORN KERNELS.

    A. How many kernels do you think there are? _____

       Work as a group to make an estimate without counting all pieces. _____

       How did you make your estimate? _____

       _____

    B. Make another estimate using the grid. _____

       Tell how you made this estimate. _____

       _____

    C. Count. Record the number. _____

       How close to the actual number were the two estimates? _____

       Was using a grid a helpful strategy? Why or why not? _____

       _____

II. CHOOSE A CONTAINER THAT YOU THINK WILL HOLD ALL THE POPPED KERNELS.

    A. Answer all the questions in part A before going on to part B.

       How much do the unpopped kernels weigh? _____

       How much do you think the popped kernels will weigh? _____

       How many minutes will the corn take to pop? _____

       How many kernels do you think will be unpopped? _____

    B. Pop the corn. How long did it take to pop the corn? _____

       Pour your popped corn into the container you chose.

       Was the container too big? Too little? Just right? _____

       How many kernels were unpopped? _____

       How much do the popped kernels weigh? _____

       Write two things you learned by doing these experiments.

       _____

       _____

       _____

NEWSPAPER SCAVENGER HUNT

Names of your team members: _____   _____

_____   _____

In a newspaper, find the following items, cut them out, and paste your examples next to the description.

1. The price of something to eat

2. A street address

3. A number that gives a size

4. A phone number

5. The date the paper was published

6. A number in a recipe

7. A number that names a distance

8. A number that names a temperature

9. A number written in words

10. The score of a game

DATA BANK

FOOD	AMOUNT	CALORIES
bran flakes	2/3 cup	90
corn flakes	1 cup	110
toasted oat cereal	2/3 cup	110
puffed wheat	1 cup	60
raisin bran	2/3 cup	120
whole milk	8 oz.	160
2 percent milk	8 oz.	145
skim milk	8 oz.	90
banana	1	100
peach	1	35
sugar	1 tablespoon	40

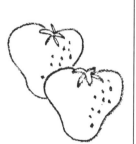

Write two problems using the data in the data bank.

Problem 1: _____

_____

_____

Problem 2: _____

_____

_____

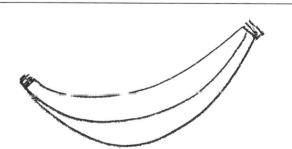

MAKING SENSE OF DATA

A spirit of investigation and exploration should permeate statistics instruction. Children's questions about the physical world can often be answered by collecting and analyzing data. After generating questions, they decide what information is appropriate and how it can be collected, displayed, and interpreted to answer their questions. The analysis and evaluation that occur as children attempt to draw conclusions about the original problem often lead to new conjectures and productive investigations. This entire process broadens children's view of mathematics.... (NCTM 1989a, p. 54)

Third-grade children are keenly aware of what others think about certain topics. This interest in others broadens and deepens as children gather and analyze opinions from a variety of people. In the following activities, children begin to acquire the techniques they need to collect and interpret data. Children will refine these skills as they move through mathematics programs that are rich in the use of statistics.

Children need experience in deciding what opinion questions they want answered as well as in collecting and presenting the data. Although students at this level probably will not conduct surveys scientifically, they will begin the process of making decisions on the basis of data.

Students should not collect all data through surveys. They need experience collecting information by using other strategies. Even straightforward research as suggested here may lead to many profitable side trips into other school subjects and other topics in mathematics.

Children sometimes have difficulty with pictographs and other graphs in which each picture or symbol stands for more than one object. But careful development here will help children make sense of units and of multiplication. For example, in the activity How Much Milk?, a gradual transition is made from one unit (half-pints) to another (gallons).

As with all the suggestions in this book, these activities do not attempt to develop all the necessary concepts or skills associated with making sense of data. They do furnish springboards for further investigations. If the children develop the questioning spirit and realize that they can answer questions in many ways—some of which are statistical—then they are well on their way to becoming mathematically literate citizens of today and tomorrow.

WHAT COLOR IS OUR FOOD?

Get ready. The purpose of this activity is to have children do research and make and interpret graphs.

Clear a space on a bulletin board or chalkboard and prepare small squares of colored construction paper to match the food colors.

Children in St. Croix brought such foods as coconuts, papayas, mangoes, and guavas to their class. This activity affords a wonderful opportunity for your students to learn more about the different cultural backgrounds of their classmates.

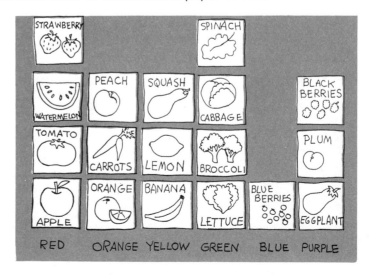